MURPHY, CARE DOG
Dogs Can Do Many Things
Thomas James

KNOWLEDGE
BOOKS

Teacher Notes:

Murphy is an Australian Shepherd. He has been trained to be a care dog. Murphy visits hospitals, schools, and aged care facilities. He is trained to let people pat him and for him to not jump or get scared. This is a story about Murphy, what he likes, and some of his adventures.

Discussion points for consideration:

1. Why do we use care dogs?

2. What is special about Murphy's fur?

3. What was Murphy trained for?

4. What does Murphy do in his free time?

Difficult words to be introduced and practiced before reading this book:

Australian, Shepherd, popular, medium, protect, loyal, woolly, tumbleweed, exactly, behaving, natural, special, hospital, quickly, therapy, uniform, beautiful, tangled, exercise, energy, healthy, carnivores, vegetable, exciting.

Contents

1. Who is Murphy?

Murphy is an Australian Shepherd. This dog breed is very popular in America. Their size is medium to big. They are very smart and can run very fast.

Australian Shepherds make very good pets. They will protect their owners and are very brave and loyal.

Murphy is a big woolly dog. He looks like a big ball of fur with legs sticking out. Or maybe a tumbleweed with a smiling face at one end!

Some people say that he looks like a little lion with his furry mane, or a tiger with strange stripes. Others ask if he wears makeup around his eyes. Murphy does not wear makeup!

2. What Are Australian Shepherds?

Murphy is a pure-bred dog. This means he is a puppy from a pure line of Australian Shepherds. This is done to keep the puppies exactly like their parents. People buy puppies knowing that this dog will be the same as the parent dogs. The puppy will have the same looks and ways of behaving.

When Murphy was bought, his new owners were given the details of his parents and grandparents. This is to prove that he is a true Australian Shepherd.

Murphy is not shaved in summer as he has two layers of fur. This provides a layer of air between the outside and inside fur. This stops the heat and cold from getting in. You do not shave this breed of dog. It can cause them to be too hot in summer and too cold in winter.

Dogs lose their heat by panting. Panting with water in their breath is how dogs cool down. Murphy stops his body from getting too hot by panting harder. He will also lay his belly on the cold floor with his legs apart.

Australian shepherds are very smart and fast. They became popular because they can herd and look after sheep and goats. There are many wild animals such as wolves, coyotes, wild dogs, and big cats that will eat sheep.

The speed of Australian shepherds means they can quickly catch up to sheep. They look to their owner who points to where the sheep need to go. The owner can also call the dog with a 'fetch' or a whistle.

Murphy is a natural working dog, just like his parents and grandparents. He guards his owners and likes to herd ducks and other animals.

'Murphy' is a common name for dogs. It comes from an Irish word that means 'sea warrior'. Murphy is also a last name for many people from Ireland. It is the most popular last name in Ireland.

Murphy was named after a special donkey who carried wounded soldiers in World War I. The donkey was brave and hard-working, and carried soldiers to the hospital.

13

Murphy is a happy, friendly, and caring dog. When he was young, everything was new for him. He could not walk up and down stairs. He was afraid of the waves at the beach. He did not know any tricks.

Murphy is brave and learnt quickly. Now he can run down the stairs and swim in the sea. He loves to learn new tricks and solve puzzles. He greets new people with a handshake or a high-five.

15

Murphy knows when it is time for breakfast each day. He rests his head on Alice's shoulder to wake her up at the right time. If she does not wake up, he licks her on the nose. That wakes her up quickly! Alice stands up and says, "Good morning, Murphy!" Then Murphy stands up tall on two feet to give her a big hug.

Joshua takes Murphy to the park to run around and chase other dogs. Sometimes Murphy finds a puddle and decides to roll around in it until he looks like a swamp monster! Joshua tells Murphy to get out of the puddle. Murphy often pretends not to hear him. Murphy loves puddles!

Murphy is twice as fast as normal dogs. All his best friends at the dog park are giant dogs. He loves running and playing with other dogs. He chases other dogs and loves being chased. He fetches the ball for a little time and then stops for a rest.

21

Murphy has long, soft fur. Joshua combs him and the old fur is brushed out. The loose hair is kept in bags to give away for spinning into mittens and beanies. Murphy's fur is soft and warm, like a wolf's fur.

Wolf fur was used by people who trekked to the North and South Poles. It was the warmest fur to use. They wore fur gloves to make sure their hands did not freeze. Dogs originally came from grey wolves. There are still many things about them which are the same.

23

3. Murphy and Friends

Murphy lives in a house with another dog called Dee. Dee is also an Australian shepherd. Murphy is older than Dee. He taught her not to be afraid of the vacuum cleaner.

Dee and Murphy play all day together and have their own special games. Dee loves to chase the ball. Sometimes Murphy will pick up the ball with his mouth and throw it into the air for Dee to catch.

After playing, Murphy and Dee like to have a carrot as a healthy snack. Carrots are good for dogs' teeth and gums.

Murphy goes for walks with Dee, Alice, and Joshua every day. During summer, the concrete path can be too hot for his paws. The best plan is to make sure he walks on the grass. They also walk in the coolest part of the day.

The nails of a dog need to be worn down. You can do this by walking your dog on stone or concrete paths. Dogs may need their nails trimmed. Use a special tool and only take small pieces. A vet can show you how to trim your dog's nails.

4. Training a Care Dog

Care dogs go to clinics, hospitals, schools, and old people's homes where people can pat, hug, and play with them. A dog can only become a care dog after doing special training. They do exams with the person in charge of them. Then they can work with their person to help other people with therapy, learning, or other things.

Murphy did therapy dog training with Alice. He passed his therapy dog exams. He now works at lots of different places with Alice.

Murphy wears a uniform when he is working. This shows people that he is a therapy dog. He knows when he is on the job. He is well-behaved and walks slowly around old and young people.

People enjoy spending time with such a beautiful and special dog. When they see Murphy, they pat him and tell him that he is a good boy. This makes his tail wag quickly from side to side.

When something very exciting happens, Murphy's whole bottom swings from left to right. His body bends like a big banana! He has a big smile on his face and is very happy.

Being a therapy dog is a lot of fun, but it is also tiring. Murphy can only work for a short time and then needs to rest. Just like us, he likes to have his free time to play and have his own fun. When Murphy finishes work, he likes to run around on beaches, sniff around the garden, and play with other dogs like Dee.

5. Feeding and Caring for Murphy

Murphy needs to be looked after too! His long fur needs washing and brushing. He gets very dirty in the mud and dirt.

A dog with long hair needs to be brushed often. This stops large pieces of hair getting tangled. These burrs of hair can rub against his skin.

All dogs need exercise. Australian Shepherds are very strong and full of energy. You must exercise these dogs every day. They love walks and it keeps them healthy. Chasing a ball is another good way to make them run fast.

Feeding your dog good food is very important. Dogs do best on raw meat and bones. Dogs are carnivores and have teeth that can chew bones and tear at meat.

Fresh cooked vegetables with some meat pieces are also good for dogs. Canned food and dried food are okay if you mix them with fresh food.

Murphy is a happy and very well-trained dog. He is always a caring dog to people. Murphy knows when you are upset or unhappy, and he will stand right beside you. It is his way of showing that he is looking after you. He is telling you not to worry or be upset. If he hears loud talking, he sometimes gets worried. He wants to give you a doggy hug.

Australian shepherds are very popular dogs. Are they the right dog for you? Here are some things to think about before getting a dog:

- Exercise – will you have time to walk or run your dog every day?

- Food – will you be able to get fresh food and meat for your dog?

- Bed – will you have somewhere warm and dry for them to sleep?

- Fencing – do you have a fence and gate to keep your dog in the yard?

Can you do all these things? Getting a dog is exciting but they need to be looked after and given lots of time and love. If you can do this, it may be time for you to get your very own dog!

Word Bank

Australian
Shepherd
popular
medium
protect
loyal
woolly
tumbleweed
exactly
behaving
natural
special
hospital
quickly
therapy
uniform
beautiful

tangled
exercise
energy
healthy
carnivores
vegetable
exciting